GW00646591

THE NEW MOVEMENTS
A Theological Introduction

by
Fr Ian Ker

*All booklets are published thanks to the
generous support of the members of the
Catholic Truth Society*

CATHOLIC TRUTH SOCIETY
PUBLISHERS TO THE HOLY SEE

CONTENTS

INTRODUCTION

The Second Vatican Council took place in the early 1960s. Like President Kennedy's death, it is probably fixed only in the memories of people over 50 years old. For many Catholics it may mean little. Some of us may remember Vatican II from childhood, in terms of changes to the Sunday morning parish Mass, but for the most part it has already escaped the experience of many as it recedes rapidly into history.

Today there remain strongly held feelings and opinions as to what the Council was meant to achieve, and how and whether it has or is being implemented. Some prophesied at the time that the next 50 to 100 years of the Church's life would revolve around the question to what extent the Council was accepted and implemented.

Why all this talk of the Council in a booklet which addresses what to many people is certainly a rather 'new' and even unusual topic: the 'new ecclesial movements' - a terminology which is rapidly becoming a part of modern catholic vocabulary. Understanding what may seem an unusual development in the history of the Church depends greatly on the lens through which we view it. On this subject there is, in a real sense, no other more valuable lens through which to understand and evaluate the new movements than the Second Vatican Council.

What are these new movements? There were over 200
of them represented in St Peter's Square at a meeting
with Pope John Paul in 1998. Some are better known
than others. They include L'Arche Communities, the
Focolare Movement, Communion and Liberation
Movement, Charismatic Renewal, the neo-Catechumenal
Communities, the Ascent Movement, Youth 2000, the
Faith Movement, to name only some and there are many,
many others. All of them share much in common, yet all
of them are quite distinguishable from one another, and
all of them claim a particular charism or service, with a
distinct proposal to make to the Church and to humanity.
Many would not describe themselves as a 'movement'
for good reason, others are 'communities' to a larger or
lesser degree. Others, while sharing the evangelical
flavour of all of them, have quite distinct constitutional
structures, such as Opus Dei. Again, most were born in
particular places, at particular times, sometimes initiated
by particular founders, lay people or priests. They devote
themselves to renewing the faith, to serving unity, the
sick, the elderly, Christian baptismal formation, evange-
lisation, particularly through the means of smaller, inti-
mate communities or groups. They nourish vocations.
Many transcend the different Christian denominations.

This new phenomenon has been monitored closely by
recent popes, since the period between the last two world
wars and up to and after the Council. Though a generali-
sation, there would seem to be some truth in the view

that as parish Church attendances have declined world-wide since the 1960s - especially of young people - so these communities and movements have emerged, quite unplanned, and flourished. They find new life and appeal. Strong criticism has been levelled in different quarters about the new ecclesial communities; again a great many Catholics and others know little about them. Similarly they have received considerable papal interest and approval. They enjoy an ever-increasing following and increasingly more bishops are expressing interest across the five continents.

For this reason the CTS offers this theological introduction by Fr Ian Ker, the first booklet in a new series on this theme. This book seeks to place the new movements in their historical, theological and ecclesiological context. Fr Ker's analysis of the Second Vatican Council, in particular the articulation between charismatic and hierarchical gifts and his belief that the Church has much to learn from the new movements in transcending the traditional laity - clergy divide makes compelling reading.

The series will contain booklets devoted to each particular 'ecclesial movement', or community, or other similar organisation. We hope it will add to the common pool of knowledge, encourage readers to find out more, and in particular to assist us all to discern 'the signs of the times'.

The founders of some of the major new Ecclesial Movements at the Pentecost meeting with Pope John Paul II in 1998. Front row from left to right: Andrea Riccardi founder of Sant'Egidio, Chiara Lubich founder of the Focolare, Kiko Arguello founder of the Neo Catechumenal Way, Jean Vanier founder of L'Arche and Mons. Luigi Giussani founder of Communion and Liberation.

THE NATURE OF THE CHURCH: *Lumen Gentium*

What model of the Church?

If you were to ask the average Catholic who the most important person in the Church is, they would almost certainly say that the pope is. If you were then to ask who the next most important people in descending order are, they would say the cardinals, bishops, then the clergy, and lastly the laity; if asked about 'religious' such as monks and nuns, they would probably be a little less sure but would almost certainly put them between the clergy and the laity.

If, however, you put the same question to a particular type of educated, middle-class Catholic, they might well reverse the order. That is to say, while acknowledging that the pope, followed by the bishops and clergy, are the leaders of the Church, this kind of Catholic might well want to introduce a reservation. For although they too would assume this 'pyramid' model of the Church, they would wish, as it were, to put it on its head. They would argue that the pope is in the same kind of position as any elected leader in being 'answerable' to those he governs. This kind of Catholic, if challenged, would explain that the Second Vatican Council decided to move away from a hierarchical Church to a more democratic kind of Church in which the laity, who constitute the vast majority of its members, would be consulted and have their voice heard. Implicitly if not explicitly, an analogy would be drawn between the laity and the electorate of a democracy to which the government is answerable.

In fact, neither of these two models of the Church was endorsed at Vatican II. There was certainly, and deliberately, a move away from the kind of primarily hierarchical Church which had dominated Catholic ecclesiology through the period of the Counter-Reformation. In so far as the Council of Trent was a reaction against the Protestant Reformation, it emphasised those elements of the Catholic tradition that were under attack, such as the ministerial priesthood and the objectivity of the sacraments. But inevitably those elements of the tradition that the Protestants wished to highlight at the expense of others tended to be downplayed or even neglected. Thus, for example, the reading of the Scriptures was discouraged because the Reformers appealed to the Bible against both tradition and the teaching authority of the Church; similarly, the priesthood of *all* the baptized was downplayed, while the various dimensions of the Eucharistic liturgy were subordinated to the priestly sacrifice of the Mass. For all its achievements and glories, then, the Tridentine Catholicism of the Counter-Reformation was not without its defects and weaknesses. The Second Vatican Council, which Pope John XXIII called both to renew the Church and to encourage Christian reunion, was naturally anxious to restore the balance.

Vatican II and *Lumen Gentium*

Vatican II was very largely a Council about the Church, about its internal components and its external relations. But presumably the most important of the documents it issued was the Constitution on the Church, otherwise referred to by its opening Latin words *Lumen Gentium*. For this contained the Council's essential teaching on the very nature of the Church. And as such, it was the most revolutionary of the Council's documents: revolutionary, not in the sense of being new, but in the literal sense of the Latin word from which it derives, of rolling back - that is, returning the Church to its original identity as defined in Scripture and the Fathers.

The key text, as one would expect, is to be found in the opening description of the fundamental nature of the Church. This, significantly in view of subsequent interpretations of the Council, was not the part of the Constitution that attracted the most attention. At the time and since, the two chapters that attracted the most interest were those on the bishops and laity. This was quite understandable. In the first place, the First Vatican Council which defined papal infallibility was never concluded because of political events in Italy. It was therefore of pressing theological urgency that the Council should take up where the previous Council had left off and produce a larger teaching about the Church, not least about the relation of the papacy to the episcopate; otherwise, there was a danger of the successor of Peter being seen as above, in the sense of separate from, the successors of the other Apostles. Secondly, since the time of Vatican I there had been a growing feeling that the Church had become far too clericalized at the expense of the laity. That was another obvious issue that the Council had to address.

Consequently, it was easy to pass over the first chapter of *Lumen Gentium*, entitled 'The Mystery of the Church', as though it were stating nothing of any great moment. This failure to realize the radical significance of what will, I suspect, prove to be the most important text of the Council in the long run, was only compounded by a mis-interpretation of the second chapter, called 'The People of God', which was and is widely believed to be about the laity, whereas in actual fact it is about all the baptized, that is, all the members of the Church. Let us, then, turn to these first two chapters in which Vatican II gave its most profound response to the call of Pope John XXIII for both Catholic renewal and Christian reunion, two goals which cannot be separated from each other.

Renewal and Reunion, the Charismatic nature of the Church

The Council could not have expressed its decision to bring the era of the Counter-Reformation to a close more decisive-ly than by defining the Church as first and foremost a 'mys-tery' and 'in the nature of sacrament'. (1) This sent a very clear ecumenical signal to the separated Eastern Orthodox Churches. Similarly, the fact that the chapter on 'The People of God' precedes chapter 3 called 'The Church is Hierarchical' makes it clear to Protestants that the Catholic Church is not first and foremost hierarchical, although it certainly is hierarchical and has a ministerial priesthood which differs in essence and not only in degree from the common priesthood of all the baptized. But the decision not to begin the Constitution with the hierarchical nature of the Church, as would have been the normal way of proceeding prior to the Council, but with the sacramental nature of the Church, was not only of great ecumenical significance but also of considerable importance for the revitalization of the Church.

This is by no means to say that the hierarchical nature of the Church is ignored in the Council's teaching on the essential nature of the Church. Far from it. But what is so striking is the way in which it is described. Having affirmed St Paul's description of the Church as the temple of the Holy Spirit, *Lumen Gentium* proceeds to say, in what may well prove to be the most radical and significant statement in all the Council's documents, that the Holy Spirit 'bestows upon her varied hierarchical and charismatic gifts'. (4)

Those words are crucial for two reasons. First, this explicit recognition, right at the beginning of the Constitution, of the inherently charismatic character of the Church is of the utmost significance. Similarly, in the

(1) For all notes see page 56.

second chapter, we read that the Holy Spirit 'distributes special graces among the faithful of every rank. By these gifts he makes them fit and ready to undertake various tasks and offices for the renewal and building up of the Church ...Whether these charisms be very remarkable or more simple and widely diffused, they are to be received with thanksgiving and consolation since they are fitting and useful for the needs of the Church.' (12) Commenting on this passage, Pope John Paul II has written that it was under the guidance of the Holy Spirit that the Second Vatican Council 'rediscovered the charismatic dimension as one of her constitutive elements'. Secondly, the fact that the charismatic dimension is so closely linked with the hierarchical dimension makes the critical point that, far from there being any opposition between the two, they are actually complementary to each other. In the same address, the Pope pointed out that the 'institutional and charismatic aspects are co-essential as it were to the Church's constitution'. (221)

Institutional and Charismatic: both gifts of the Spirit

It is usually assumed that the charismatic and institutional are diametrically opposed to each other. But, when we speak of the institutional Church, we are really referring to the three-fold order of bishop, priest, and deacon, those holy orders which are conferred by a sacrament. But like other sacraments, this sacrament depends upon the action of the Holy Spirit and cannot be created by the Church by herself. And so the fundamental structure or institution of the Church is not institutional in the sense of being man-made but is itself charismatic in the sense of being a gift of the Spirit. When, then, *Lumen Gentium* says that the Spirit confers both hierarchic and charismatic gifts on the Church, it is not contrasting them as though one comes from the Spirit and the other from man: for the reality is that both come from the Spirit. The ministerial priesthood is therefore strictly charismatic and not institutional in the usual sense of the word.

The hierarchic and charismatic gifts of the Spirit, then, are meant to complement not oppose each other. The Council's vision is of two dimensions making together a whole. And this wholeness calls for another point to be made about these first two fundamental chapters of the Constitution of the Church. For it is striking how the Church is viewed as one organic communion. If the average Catholic, for instance, were asked to describe the membership of the Church, they would almost certainly reply that the Church consists of clergy and laity (and monks and nuns, they might add). It is noticeable, however, that *Lumen Gentium*, avoids altogether speaking in terms of clerical and lay membership of the Church in these two initial chapters, where it sets out its fundamental definition of the Church. Certainly, there are succeeding chapters on clergy, laity, and religious, but here at the outset there is no attempt to divide the Church into its separate components; instead, the Church is seen as an organic whole, as the one Body of Christ. Although there is 'a diversity of members and functions', again it is emphasised that there 'is only one Spirit', even if he gives 'different gifts'. Having divided these gifts into hierarchic and charismatic, chapter I goes on to state unequivocally that: 'Among these gifts the primacy belongs to the grace of the apostles to whose authority the Spirit himself subjects even those who are endowed with charisms.'(7) But although the hierarchic nature of the Church is clearly stated, the words 'clergy' and 'laity' are avoided.

Common priesthood of the faithful

Similarly, in chapter II, the laity and clergy are spoken of as 'the common priesthood of the faithful and the ministerial or hierarchical priesthood'; but, although ' they differ essentially and not only in degree', they 'are none the less ordered one to another; each in its own proper way shares in the one priesthood of Christ'. So again, there is diversity and variety but also unity and wholeness rather than division and separation. Because the Church is 'in the nature of sacrament', the 'organic structure' of this 'priestly community is brought into operation through the sacraments'(10-11). Consequently, the hierarchy and clergy have a strictly sacramental place in the organic structure, namely, through the particular sacrament that pertains to them, the sacrament of Holy Orders, which is listed sixth among the seven sacraments. Of course, the Council didn't intend to devalue the sacrament by placing it there; in fact, some may object that it comes before the sacrament of marriage. But what the Council did wish to emphasise is that the members of the Church are not first and foremost either clergy or laity but simply Christians who all initially receive the three sacraments of initiation, baptism, confirmation, and eucharist, and who would normally also receive the sacraments of penance and anointing in the course of their Christian lives. Having defined the sacramental life that all Christians share in common, the Constitution only then goes on to speak of the remaining two sacraments that some or many but not all Christians receive.

Why do I labour this point? Because the Council was recovering a much more Biblical model of the Church than the one that prevailed before Vatican II, and indeed, sadly, than the one that has emerged since, which, as I have already indicated, bears signs of a quite alien secular influence. Pre-Vatican II clericalism encouraged both anti-clericalism on the one hand and on the other an undue deference to the clerical state and a depreciation of the lay state. But while the pendulum has since certainly swung sharply in the opposite direction to a new kind of laicism, it is remarkable how the same assumptions about the nature of the Church have persisted. It is still widely taken for granted that the clergy are the most important or most powerful members of the Church, even if they are now no longer deferred to as before.

Secular models not applicable to the Church

This perception provokes two inconsistent reactions. One is to insist, as I have already mentioned, that the hierarchical Church should be answerable, rather like governments in a democracy are answerable to the electorate, to the so-called laity - in particular, to those members of the laity who are anxious to sit on Church commissions and committees where it is believed that the important decisions are taken. The other is to call for women and married men to be ordained so as to make access to ordination as open as possible. Otherwise, it is felt that only a section of the Church can be involved in what is referred to usually as 'decision-making'. Linked with this is the pressure for what has been called the clericalization of the laity, whereby as many of the laity as possible take upon themselves clerical roles associated with the sacramental ministry. The thinking is that even if one cannot be a priest at least one can get a foothold in the sanctuary, which will give one some share in the power which the clerical state is assumed to bestow. Naturally, there are perfectly desirable and legitimate ways in which lay people can and sometimes have to assist the clergy in their ministry and which have been approved by the Church. But what is quite foreign to the model of the Church set before us in *Lumen Gentium* is the assumption that the Church is essentially institutional in the sense that the fulfilment of baptism is sacramental ministry. To assume this, albeit implicitly, is to encourage exactly the sort of 'them and us' mentality which characterized the clerical pre-Vatican II Church, even though the balance of power is felt to have shifted or to need shifting.

The Marian dimension

After all, when we talk about 'power' in the Church we are not, or should not be, talking about the kind of power that the secular world understands. For what is the 'power' that the primary sacrament of baptism confers? It is, of course, the empowerment by the Holy Spirit, who enables the baptized to share in the divine life of the Trinity, and who also bestows on the baptized 'varied hierarchic and charismatic gifts'. Under the influence of the Holy Spirit, let us not forget, a woman took the 'decision' which altered the whole course of history. I am referring, of course, to the Blessed Virgin Mary who said 'yes' to the incarnation but who was not called by her Son to be one of his apostles. It was one of those apostles, true, who made, again under the influence of the Spirit, the crucial affirmation about who Christ was, and who consequently was placed at the head of the apostles. But

obviously, he could have made no such 'decision' without the prior 'decision' of Mary. As the *Catechism of the
Catechism of the Catholic Church* says, the Marian dimension of the
Church is prior to the Petrine, a point which is by no
means irrelevant to the question of women's ordination.
Or again, if we ask who the most important apostle was,
a question Jesus discouraged on a well-known occasion,
we would have to specify: important in what way? In
terms of hierarchy, the answer is clearly Peter. But there
is something that precedes even hierarchy in the church
and that is love, since, as the apostle John, who repre-
sents the principle of love and who was closest and
therefore most important personally to Jesus, declares,
God is love. Indeed, at the end of John's gospel, when
the risen Lord reminds Peter of his pastoral mission, he
asks him three times, to the first pope's discomfort,
whether he loves him.

If we look at the Church in history, would we want to
say that the most important or powerful of its members
must be the popes? Surely not, for not only have there
been popes who have dishonoured the petrine office, but
what then are we to say about the great saints, not least
those whose particular charisms have had great influence
on the Church's life? St Benedict and St Francis of Assisi
hugely influenced the development of the Western
Church, but neither was even a priest. And yet their importance cannot be overestimated. Similarly, in our own time

the decision Mother Theresa of Calcutta took to leave her teaching order and work among the destitute was presumably as important a 'decision' that any member of the Church took in the twentieth century, and one that was to give her great spiritual 'power' throughout the world, on a scale that very few priests or bishops could even dream of. But even to talk in such terms shows how absurd it is to apply secular categories to the Church.

Lumen Gentium makes it absolutely clear that the Holy Spirit leads and sanctifies the Church and its members not only by means of the ordained ministry. Vital as the ministry of the clergy, whether sacramental or pastoral or teaching, is for the life of the Church, chapter II states roundly that it is 'not only' through these 'sacraments' and 'ministrations' that the Spirit works. For the Spirit 'also distributes special graces among the faithful of every rank', in other words, not only among the clergy and religious but among all the baptized. And 'Whether these charisms be very remarkable or more simple and widely diffused, they are to be received with thanksgiving... since they are fitting and useful for the needs of the Church.' (12)

A Church made up of the baptized

It is this recovery of the charismatic dimension, which was inevitably neglected in the old pre-Vatican II Church, that has tended to be sidelined because of a new preoccupation with the laity as opposed to the clergy. After all, let us not forget that the word 'lay' is a negative word, meaning somebody who is not clerical. The word although not the preoccupation goes back to the early Church, since clearly there is a place and a time for the distinction. But we know what the implications are of using the word in secular contexts: 'I am only a layman,' we say when faced with someone with professional expertise that we do not possess. When, therefore, we describe all the baptized (apart, perhaps, from religious) as non-priests, we are in effect saying something rather reductive, as though anyone who is not in holy orders is only an amateur Christian. And it not only ignores the charismatic dimension but it fuels the kind of discontents I have indicated above. Of course, it *is* a perfectly factual description *if* we choose to consider all the baptized from the point of view of holy orders. But by looking at the baptized always in that perspective, we necessarily downgrade the charisms.

To take a couple of secular examples: in the society in which we live there is a great deal of preoccupation with gender and race. Now while there are indeed occasions when it is very helpful to know whether somebody is a man or woman or what colour they are, it is not healthy or helpful always to be thinking of human beings in terms of such exclusive catagories. Margaret Thatcher is a woman and that is certainly not an irrelevant fact about her, but even more important from another equally valid point of view is that she is a politician. From that point of view, she is like a number of men and unlike a great many women. More fundamentally, if we think of the human race as consisting of men and women, we may forget that the human race actually consists of human beings first and foremost, and that before any distinctions all human beings possess a common humanity - which is actually the most important thing about them.

In the same way, if we talk too much about clergy and laity we may forget that the Church actually consists of baptized Christians, who all share the same Holy Spirit through baptism. This is where *Lumen Gentium* starts from and where we should always begin before we start considering what distinctions there are between Christians. And equally, like *Lumen Gentium*, we should not immediately then emphasise the clerical-lay distinction, but rather remember that the Holy Sprit bestows 'varied hierarchic and charismatic gifts'. This keeps both the hierarchic and the charismatic dimensions not only in view but, just as important, in close association as coming from one and the same source. This has the effect not only of ensuring that the charismatic dimension is not swallowed by the hierarchic dimension, and so reducing membership of the Church to clergy and laity, but of protecting the clergy from the clericalism which inevitably leads to the anti-clericalism of the pre-Vatican II Church and to the laicism of the post-Vatican II Church.

Pentecost 1998 the Pope meets with leaders and members of the Ecclesial Movements.

HISTORICAL PERSPECTIVE

Unexpected newness of the movements

It is time to return to the address of Pope John Paul II in which he spoke of the Church's rediscovery of the charismatic dimension at Vatican II. This address was given on the eve of Pentecost 1998, when the Pope met with delegates to the World Congress of the Ecclesial Movements. Two years earlier, again on the eve of Pentecost, the Pope in a homily had said, 'One of the gifts of the Spirit to our time is undoubtedly the flourishing of the ecclesial movements which right from the beginning of my pontificate I have continued to indicate as a source of hope for the Church and for man.'(9) The 1998 meeting was not the first such meeting: similar international meetings of the ecclesial movements - and, we should add, communities - had taken place in 1981, 1987, and 1991. But the 1998 meeting was the first one organized by the Holy See and the first to meet with the Pope. In order to emphasise this papal endorsement, the Pope called the event 'truly unprecedented'. He went on to define what he meant by a movement: 'charisms are communicative and give rise to that "spiritual affinity among persons" and to that friendship in Christ which is the origin of "movements". The passage from the original charism to the movement happens through the mysterious attraction that the founder holds for all those who become involved in his spiritual experience.' The Pope acknowledged that the 'unexpected newness' of the movements has sometimes proved 'even disruptive', with 'presumptions and excesses on the one hand, and on the other ... numerous prejudices and reservations'. But the Pope was confident that the movements were now ready to move to 'ecclesial maturity', in other words to taking their formal place within the community of the Church. (220, 222)

It is very important to note how careful the Pope is to use the word 'ecclesial' in referring to the movements. He had not always been so precise or perhaps there has been an evolution in his own understanding on this point. In his apostolic exhortation of 1988, *Christifideles Laici*, from which he quoted above, he spoke rather of lay communities and movements. The Pope carefully now avoids doing that, but it is still very common to refer to them as lay movements, although that, one is tempted to say, is precisely what they are not - even though obviously the majority of their members will be lay. For what is so novel and striking - although *Lumen Gentium*'s definition of the Church should make it much less strange - is that the new movements contain bishops, clergy, religious, as well as lay people.

But here three qualifications need to be made. First, in these new communities and movements, there are so-called lay people who assume such a degree of commitment to the particular charism, often involving what normally we would call consecrated life through promising or vowing chastity, obedience, and poverty, that they are in fact quasi-religious, even though they cannot, at present at least, be formally recognized as such under the existing categories of canon law. For even canon law has to follow the Spirit rather than the other way round! Second, while there are vocations from the laity within these movements to the diocesan and religious priesthood, there are also priests ordained specifically *for* the particular movement, although again this presents problems from the point of view of the existing canon law. Third, the movements are not ageist, that is, they include the very elderly as well as children, which again sets them apart from the so-called laity of the post-Vatican II Church, who would not normally include either of these two age-groups, whether for what is called 'collaborative ministry' or for the committees and bureaucracy of the institutional Church.

True community of the baptized

The novelty and originality, then, of these new associations is that they really do represent that organic and unified community of the baptized that we read about both in the New Testament and in *Lumen Gentium* - at least in the first two chapters where the Church's nature is defined, [even if the following chapters do deal separately with the different components of Church membership in the usual accepted way]. This bringing together of all the baptized within one community and for a common mission is hugely significant. It is so unlike what Catholics have become accustomed to. For we might say that division rather than unity has been the practice, if not the theory. Catholics understand particular associations for particular groups of the laity, like the Children of Mary, for example. They assume that priests too are grouped separately from other baptized Christians, whether in the presbyterate of the diocese or a religious order or congregation. The only exception in the case of the latter was the existence of lay brothers, who, I think it is true to say, were regarded as second-class members, that is to say, men who were unable for whatever reason to proceed to the priesthood. This was and still usually is the case even in monasteries, where one might expect the vocation to monastic life to be so obviously paramount that the ordained priesthood would be seen as secondary to the monastic charism.

But even in saying 'secondary', one risks the possibility of misunderstanding. For in a Church where priesthood was and still is seen as the ultimate fulfilment of baptism, to suggest that there might be a charism that could take precedence would suggest that the monk is more 'important' than a priest, which would be regarded as an impossibility.

And, of course, there is no question of implying any such thing: in the words of the well-known dictum, such comparisons are odious. They are indeed very odious, for they amount to a denial of the charismatic dimension, or at least to it being subsumed to the hierarchic dimension. As we have seen, it is certainly true that the charismatic dimension of the Church requires the authentication and regulation of the hierarchical dimension. For among the gifts of the Spirit, 'the primacy belongs to the grace of the apostles to whose authority the Spirit himself subjects even those who are endowed with charisms.' But when St Paul defines the membership of the Church in a famous passage, he doesn't say, 'apostles first and then the laity', but rather: 'Now you together are Christ's body; but each of you is a different part of it. In the Church, God has given the first place to apostles, the second to prophets, the third to teachers; after them, miracles, and after them the gift of healing; helpers, good leaders, those with many languages.' (*I Cor. 12:27-28*) It is this same vision of a hierarchical but also charismatic Church that *Lumen Gentium* rediscovered and that has now taken concrete, living form in the new ecclesial movements.

New movements in the Church's history

In his opening message to the 1998 congress, the Pope recognized that the term 'movement' 'certainly cannot exhaust or capture the wealth of forms aroused by the life-giving-creativity of the Spirit of Christ', still 'it does indicate a concrete ecclesial reality with predominantly lay membership, a journey of faith and a Christian witness which bases its own pedagogical method on a precise charism given to the person of the founder in specific circumstances and ways'.(18) In a highly theological address, Cardinal Joseph Ratzinger, the Prefect of the Congregation for the Doctrine of the Faith, offered a very similar definition. Setting the contemporary phenomenon of the movements within a larger historical perspective, he pointed out how the history of the Church shows that at certain periods there have been widespread movements of the Spirit which have profoundly changed and renewed the Church. The Cardinal referred to the Franciscan awakening in the thirteenth century' as 'probably' providing 'the clearest instance of what a movement is': 'movements generally derive their origin from a charismatic leader and take shape in concrete communities, inspired by the life of their founder; they attempt to live the Gospel anew, in its totality, and recognise the Church without hesitation as the ground of their life without which they could not exist.' (47-8)

But there have been other no less significant spiritual movements in the course of the Church's history. And Cardinal Ratzinger linked them to the universal as opposed to the local dimension of the Church's life. Thus, in the first instance, when the universal ministry of the apostles - who were not bishops of local churches but apostles of the whole Church - died out and was absorbed by the local episcopal ministry in the course of the second century, already as early as the third century the monastic movement appeared. But this retreat into the desert 'was a deliberate abandonment of the firmly established structure of the local Church'. Spiritually, it was, of course, 'a flight from a Christianity that was progressively adapting itself to the needs of secular life, in order to follow uncompromisingly in the footsteps of Christ'. This zeal is the hall-mark of all the movements in the Church's history, but Cardinal Ratzinger also points to the way in which the monastic charism represented a spiritual alternative to the pastoral ministry of the episcopate and clergy of the local churches: '... the monastic movement created a new centre of life that did not abolish the local ecclesial structure of the post-apostolic Church, but that did not simply coincide with it either.' Ratzinger is careful not to imply that the institutional and charismatic became totally separated: instead, monasticism was 'active ... as a life-giving force, a kind of reservoir from which the local Church could draw truly spiritual clergy in whom the fusion of institution and charism was constantly renewed'. (38-9) Far from being unique, Ratzinger argues, monasticism was only the first of several major spiritual movements that have renewed both the universal mission of the Church and the vitality of the local churches.

The role of the papacy

For, far from being shut up in its monasteries, from the end of the sixth century monasticism became a great missionary movement with St Patrick in Ireland and St Augustine in England. The papacy had not created the monastic movement, but the popes saw its missionary potential and became its chief supporters. Ratzinger now makes another very important point: because the pope is not merely bishop of the local church of Rome, but has a universal ministry in a unique way that no local bishop has, he has a special interest in encouraging movements like monasticism which go beyond the scope and structure of the local church and have a special apostolic dynamism.

The next most important wave or movement of the Spirit came with St Francis of Assisi and St Dominic in the thirteenth century. Francis recalled the Church to evangelical poverty and renunciation, but this went hand-in-hand with evangelization, and the friars became evangelists beyond the frontiers of Christendom. Conflict with the local institutional church was inevitable, and when this came to a head at the University of Paris between the secular clergy and the new mendicant orders, it was the Dominican St Thomas Aquinas who defended the new evangelizing movement against the institutional *status quo*. And Thomas makes more explicit what was already present in monasticism - that the religious life means not only embracing chastity, poverty, and obedience, but also the universal proclamation of the Gospel. This dramatic episode in the history of the Church shows how the self-enclosed local church could not tolerate this irruption of new spiritual life, whereas, Ratzinger points out, it was again the papacy, with its universal ecclesial ministry, that supported the new movement of the Spirit, with all its enormous apostolic potential. And, significantly, he adds, 'all this gave a great boost to the development of the doctrine of primacy', since the petrine office 'was now understood anew in the light of its apostolic roots'. (43)

The Jesuits

If the thirteenth century was the hour of the friars, the sixteenth saw the advent of the Jesuits. With half of Europe lost to the Protestant Reformation, the Society of Jesus was exactly what the Church so sorely needed at the time - a highly mobile force of well -educated and disciplined priests, explicitly at the disposal of the pope. Unlike the monks and the friars, the Jesuits were intended to be above all a priestly order, meant in fact to be model priests, at a time when the secular priesthood was at a low ebb. What the Church then desperately needed was education, both for the laity and the clergy. It was the Jesuits who became the great apologists against Protestantism. Like the monks and friars, they were responsible for a great missionary expansion through the newly discovered lands of America, Africa, and Asia. But they also fought to revive Catholicism, often with considerable success, in the parts of Europe that been lost to the Reformers. Their novelty was bound to arouse suspicion and antagonism: here were priests who were not tied to the cloister but resembled the secular clergy in celebrating the divine office not in common but privately, as well as not being committed to community life like the monks and friars. It was a new form of religious life that suited the times. But because of its novelty it aroused the same kind of opposition that another Spanish movement was to arouse in the twentieth century. Indeed, the accusations against Opus Dei in our own time remarkably resemble the traditional complaints against the Jesuits. (In passing, we might note that, ecclesiologically, Opus Dei has much in common with the new movements, not least in its understanding that there are charisms which are not necessarily orientated at all towards the ministerial priesthood.)

Vehicles for implementing Councils

After Vatican II there was much talk of what was called 'implementing' the Council, and I think it is fair to say that the bishops, who had after all been the visible participants in the Council, generally assumed that the primary responsibility for this implementation lay with them. They took it for granted that it was up to them to ensure that the reforms of Vatican II were put into effect in their dioceses. There is a curious irony in that, because it was these very same bishops who had voted for the Constitution *Lumen Gentium* who now seemed often to forget that they had been responsible for approving what Pope John Paul II clearly regards as one of the most significant achievements of the Council, the rediscovery of the charismatic dimension of the Church. At General Councils the Catholic Church believes that the Holy Spirit is powerfully present, but the Holy Spirit doesn't guarantee the bestowal of charisms on bishops at Councils. There may be very charismatic bishops who play a crucial role in the way conciliar teachings enter into the life-blood of the Church; a very obvious example would be St Charles Borromeo at the time of the Council of Trent. But for the Tridentine reforms truly to take root, more was required than outstanding bishops. Indeed, we can surely say that the Tridentine Church, the Church of the Counter-Reformation, could hardly have existed without, in particular, the charism of St Ignatius Loyola. The Society of Jesus was founded five years before that Council began its lengthy deliberations. And not only did Jesuit theologians play a crucial role in the proceedings - for we should never think that Councils happen only through the Church's hierarchy - but without the Jesuits would the decrees of Trent ever have had any real chance of profoundly changing the life of the Church?

The Jesuits were to be the first of many similar religious orders, as well as congregations, of both men and women, a phenomenon that greatly increased in the nineteenth century with the emergence of new missionary initiatives, particularly involving women. This fresh spate of movements didn't arouse the same kind of controversy as the previous movements, for, as Ratzinger points out, they were concerned with evangelization in overseas lands and not with the internal renewal of the Church. In actual fact, this new movement of the Spirit did indirectly help the local churches by highlighting the need to propagate the gospel.

Signs of the times

We come now to the twentieth century. And perhaps it is worth noting at the outset a very negative sign of the times, for it helps to throw light on what John Paul II clearly regards as the most positive sign of the times. I refer to the sudden and quite unexpected decline, even demise, of precisely that form of religious life that has so dominated the life of the Church since the sixteenth century, namely, the so-called 'active' form, of which the Society of Jesus was the most prominent example and indeed the inspiration and model for other later orders. The intense individualism of the Ignatian charism that enabled priests to go to the ends of the world, free of the constraints of both the cloister and the choir, is now proving to be the least attractive form of religious life today among the young. True, in some cases, especially in the women's orders, the particular charisms that led to their being founded were closely bound up with a special apostolate, such as teaching or nursing, for which there is no longer the same kind of need. In these cases, total extinction may indeed be inevitable. But the striking fact remains that the Society of Jesus, which was the pre-eminent form of religious life in the Church from the middle of the sixteenth to the middle of the twentieth century (apart from its period of suppression), is now attracting significantly fewer vocations than older orders like the Benedictines and Dominicans. This decline is shared by other similar active orders and congregations where community life has never been important and where there has been no emphasis on communal prayer - but rather the opposite, in the interest of their members being as disposable and mobile as possible for the service of the Church.

It is striking to find the theologian Karl Rahner, himself a Jesuit, saying in 1983 that, whereas his generation were 'spiritually ... individualists ... in a spirituality of the future the element of brotherly spiritual communion, of a spirituality lived together, may play a more decisive role, and ... slowly but surely we must continue our way along this road'. (97) These prophetic words were quoted at the 1998 congress. And we might add another factor that has adversely affected active orders like the Jesuits - the decline in the sense of *esprit de corps* in modern culture. For, while a younger generation wants to belong to and to identify with a particular community, there is no longer the same pride in belonging to an institution like an order, as there would have been for Rahner and earlier generations.

CHARISMS AND COUNCILS

Inspirations of the Holy Spirit

We should now ask: what is the relation between councils and charisms? Certainly, if the Jesuits had not already existed, Trent could hardly have decreed the Ignatian charism. For neither councils nor popes nor bishops can decree charisms which are given solely by the Holy Spirit. Equally, in the case of the new ecclesial movements, some of which also pre-dated the Second Vatican Council, neither that council nor the bishops responsible for (as perhaps they assumed too readily) implementing it could bring into being these movements which the present Pope and his predecessor Paul VI have discerned to be the work of the Spirit. However, just as Christ was incarnate in a particular place and at a particular time and in particular circumstances, so too the Holy Spirit operates not in a void but in a historical context. As Cardinal Ratzinger puts it, 'apostolic movements appear in ever new forms in history - necessarily so, because they are the Holy Spirit's answer to the ever changing situations in which the Church lives'. (46) And so it is no surprise to find that, just as the Society of Jesus was like an answer to the prayers of the council fathers at Trent, so too the new ecclesial movements remarkably embody in concrete, living form the new - or rather very old because scriptural and patristic - ecclesiology of those first two fundamental chapters of *Lumen Gentium*. Naturally, this is not to imply that any of the founders of these movements and communities - some of which pre-dated the Council anyway - was directly inspired by reading these basic texts of the Constitution on the Church, any more than Ignatius Loyola knew what the Council of Trent was to decree. The Holy Spirit doesn't, of course, work in that kind of human way. Still, the Spirit does respond to the circumstances in which the Church finds herself at particular times.

If, therefore, we wish to understand the context in which the Spirit has inspired so many men and women to live out their Christian vocation in such radically new ways, we need to remember the original decision - a truly charismatic rather than hierarchical decision - by Pope John XXIII to call a council which would both renew the Catholic Church and foster Christian reunion. For the Council was to be a council about the Church and in its central teaching about the essential nature of the Church it provided an ecclesiology that answered Pope John's call in the most radical of ways because it went back to the roots of the Church in the first centuries.

Movements confirm Vatican II

In his message to the 1998 congress Pope John Paul II, referring to Pope John's dream of a new Pentecost for the Church, called the movements 'one of the most significant

Kiko Arguello and Chiara Lubich, founders of the Neo Catechumenal Way and Focolare respectively, both groups which sprang up before Vatican II but in its spirit.

fruits of that springtime in the Church which was fore-
told by the Second Vatican Council, but which unfortunately has often been hampered by the spread of secular-
ization'. (16) The Pope sees the movements as not only
inspired by the Spirit - as all apostolic movements in the
Church are - but as reflecting clearly the teaching of
Vatican II on the charismatic dimension of the Church,
as well as its inseparability from the hierarchical dimension of the Church which also comes from the same
Holy Spirit. The movements evidence the organic unity
and communion of the Church in which all the baptized
share in the same Spirit, who, however, gives them different charisms and gifts.

As Hans Urs von Balthasar has pointed out, in the history of the Church charisms come 'like a bolt of lightning
from the blue, destined to illuminate a single and
original point of God's will for the Church in a given
time'. (86) They can't be either foreseen or determined
even by the hierarchy, even though they require hierarchical authentication.

Holiness of the Baptized to be realised

Lumen Gentium stressed the organic unity of the Church,
not only in the sense of beginning with the unity if diversity of the baptized, rather than the hierarchical divisions
between them, but also by commencing in its very first
article with the enormously significant affirmation that

'the Church, in Christ, is in the nature of sacrament - a sign and instrument, that is, of communion with God and of unity among all men'. As Mgr Piero Coda, a theologian belonging to the Focolare movement, put it at the 1998 congress, the Church sacramentally makes Christ present not only by preaching, sacraments, and pastoral ministry, but also 'in the sense that she is, as community of the disciples who live the "new" commandment both among each other and in their relations with everybody, the sign and the instrument of the meeting with the risen Christ for the men and women of our time'. It is what he calls the 'peculiarity' of the ecclesial movements that they make 'the presence of Christ felt through the communion lived by his disciples'. Anyone reading those pregnant words can hardly help being reminded of the famous description of the early Christians, 'how they love each other'. In a secularised world that may be the best way of preaching the gospel, by showing our contemporaries how true communion between human beings can be realized through the power of the risen Christ. The early Church didn't have missionary orders to spread the faith in the Roman empire, but it had itself, the communion of the baptized filled with the Spirit.

Coda points too to another aspect of the rediscovery of the Church as mystery, the fact that the Church is not only the Body but also the Bride of Christ, who, as *Lumen Gentium* states,' is regenerated by the gift of self of the Bridegroom, and called to clothe herself in the nuptial vestment of holiness'. But this aspect of the Church's mystery is also realized by the movements, where holiness 'is not reserved for an elite [i.e. clergy and religious] but open to the whole people of God'.(94) For after all, holiness is the only 'power' that should matter to the baptized Christian who is empowered by the Spirit. Other kinds of power are there, as Jesus pointed out to Peter, only for the purpose of propagating the love of God. Much since the Council has been said and written about the rights of the laity and the importance of involving them in the decision-making structures of the Church, and it is certainly true that proper methods and possibilities of consultation should exist. But a very great deal less has been said about Vatican II's call for holiness among all the baptized. Again, it is to the new ecclesial movements and communities that we must look for a realization of this vision. After all, there is no point whatsoever in all the structures and meetings in the world unless holiness is the ultimate goal. But who can honestly say that Christian love has informed and stimulated much of the confrontations and contestations that have sadly so dominated the life of the Church since the Second Vatican Council? Still, councils are times of great controversy and upheaval in the Church, and it is perhaps no surprise that while the media were concentrating their attention elsewhere, the Spirit was quietly at work out of sight of most of the institutional Church.

Speaking of structures, it is worth noting Piero Coda's point that, while it is true that charisms have always been accepted *de facto* as part of the Church's life, in *Lumen Gentium* they are 'recognised in a structural way as a necessary condition for the self-expression of the Church as communion in the present phase of salvation.'(94) And he emphasises John Paul II's address in 1998 on, significantly, the vigil of Pentecost, when the Pope spoke of *Lumen Gentium's* rediscovery of the charismatic dimension 'as a constituent part' of the Church.

Ecclesiality of the Movements

In his important study, Coda goes on to speak of another 'constituent feature of the movements', namely their 'ecclesiality', an aspect I have already touched on. To describe them as lay movements is not simply factually inaccurate but also ecclesiologically false; for 'The new movements are constitutionally open (by virtue of their original charism) to all the vocations and to all the states of life present in the People of God.' And so the description of them as 'lay' movements is wholly 'reductive', since they not only in fact but in theory embrace all the baptized. To insist, therefore, on their correct description is not mere academic pedantry, as many might think on the ground that, after all, they do (inevitably) include more laity than clergy and religious. Coda calls their common classification as lay movements 'inertia of reflection'. (95) But I think we can be more precise than that: the misdescription reflects that very ecclesiology of clergy on the one side and laity on the other, from which the first two chapters of *Lumen Gentium* sought to free the Church. The movements are 'ecclesial' or church movements precisely because they share the same ecclesiology of organic wholeness.

The point is too important not to risk the danger of labouring it. For it is not just that the movements do in fact include priests and religious within them - although this certainly shows that 'the charism that lies at the origin of the movements is not in conflict, for example, with the spirituality and ministerial obligations of the priesthood nor with the charism of the consecrated life aroused and shaped according to the various spiritualities'. But, more fundamentally, the movements represent the concrete real-ization - undecreed, unplanned as they are by any councils or synods or committees - of that idea of *communio* or communion that lies at the heart of Vatican II's under-standing of the Church. What we see in them, in Coda's words again, is the actuality of communion among the baptized, whereby 'the equal baptismal dignity and the complementarity of the various vocations, ministries and charisms' are made authentically possible 'in an organi-cally and hierarchically structured communion'. (96)

MOVEMENTS AND EVANGELISATION

We must now turn to another aspect of the movements, which takes us back to the primary reason for the traditional papal encouragement and support of new apostolic and spiritual movements in the Church: their missionary potential. Evangelization was not a major theme of the Second Vatican Council, although there was a decree on the Church's missionary activity. However, in 1974 Pope Paul VI called for a new evangelization in *Evangelii Nuntiandi*, a theme that has constantly recurred during the pontificate of John Paul II.

Problems facing the Church

In the secularised countries in the West, it is recognized on all sides that there is an urgent need to find effective ways of preaching the gospel, not least to young people. Indeed, there is the pressing pastoral problem of how to sustain the faith even of those who do attend Mass. In the pre-Vatican II Church there were well-established methods of effectively ensuring to a considerable degree the continuing active membership of the Church from cradle to grave. The parish, reinforced by a Catholic school system, to a large extent staffed by nuns, priests, and brothers, was able to provide a context in which the faith of the Catholic community was largely sustained. At least that was the case in the rural parts of Catholic Europe (except where dechristianization, especially in areas of France since the French Revolution, had long been established), although the urbanization that followed the industrial revolution had long been posing a very serious pastoral problem in the cities. In countries like Britain and the United States, where Catholics were a minority, the crisis in the urban parts of continental Europe had been to a considerable degree averted because a largely immigrant Catholic population effectively formed its own enclosed, ghetto-like community where the Church was the focal point of social identity. This means of preserving a distinctly Catholic identity was not open to the Church in the so-called Catholic cities of Europe where the vast majority of the inhabitants were nominally Catholic - except in countries like Ireland and Poland where Catholicism went hand-in-hand with nationalism and cultural identity.

Today, however, the problems that had long faced the Church in Europe - from which English-speaking bishops at Vatican II were able still to feel comfortably insulated - have now become a reality for the Church in cities like Boston and Liverpool where an immigrant Irish population has over the years gradually lost its distinctly Irish and Catholic identity thanks to inter-marriage and immersion in the indigenous culture. There are obviously many aspects of this crisis that cannot be discussed here - including the dramatic effects of the 1960s revolution.

But it is not irrelevant to note that the decline in membership of the active orders of priests, brothers, and nuns, who specialized in teaching, has greatly exacerbated the situation. And at this point one should add that the unfashionable individualism of these orders is also, of course, something that affects the diocesan clergy, where there has also been a great decline in vocations, as well as a loss of confidence in mission.

Pockets of hope

But one does not need to be a religious sociologist, on the other hand, to note and appreciate the reasons for the success, by way of marked contrast, of certain groups in both the Protestant and Catholic Churches. For, whereas the alarming signs of decline in both communities are self-evident, there are two striking exceptions. The one is the growth of the so-called 'house' and 'community' churches among Protestants, and the other is the extraordinary emergence of the new movements and communities, particularly in the Latin countries, in the Catholic Church. In English-speaking and northern European countries, the movements are much less strong and less well-established, a fact that explains the meteoric rise of vocations to the priesthood in dechristianized Rome, for example, where the new movements are flourishing, as compared, say, with Catholic Dublin where the old clericalism remains strong and where priestly vocations have sharply declined.

Community preaches and incarnates the Gospel

The incontestable fact that both the house and community churches in the Protestant denominations - as well as the Evangelical equivalent of the Catholic movements such as the Christian Union which is very successful in schools and universities - and the new communities and movements in the Catholic Church show practically the only signs of growth, indeed almost the sole cases where more or less severe decline is not taking place, has both a negative and a positive aspect. By negative aspect, I mean that it is in such contexts that today's Christians, living in a fiercely secular not to say pagan society, find the support for their faith as they all too often don't find it in the institutional parishes. But there is also the very positive consideration that it is precisely through these closely-knit faith-communities that it becomes possible to preach the gospel to the unbelieving. Where once it was enough to preach to preach to people who still retained a substantial degree of belief in Christianity but whose practice of the faith was defective, in the contemporary world it is increasingly necessary to *show* people experientially that the gospel 'works', that is to say, that the love of Christ makes possible a new kind of happiness and hope. Missionaries to pagan countries have traditionally made their preaching 'incarnate' by means of hospitals and schools. But in a secular society the gospel comes alive and real to people when it is accompanied by, 'incarnate' in a community context. In other words, the gospel provides a supply for a deeply felt need - the dreadful lack of community in an urban environment where the old family and village structures no longer exist and where people are forced to lead highly individualistic, isolated lives in an alienating environment. Any kind of community will seem attractive, as the sects and cults have unfortunately found. But where genuinely loving Christian community is offered and where this is inseparable from clear and firm faith in redemption and salvation, then what would otherwise be mere words and abstract theories to the secularised imagination become concrete and compelling and real. Again, this is only a revolutionary change insofar as it marks a return to the way in which the early Church in fact grew. There were no missionary orders then, as I have already remarked, but there were vibrant faith-communities which won both the hearts and minds of the pagans of the day. Without exaggerating too much, one can perhaps say that for our dechristianized contemporaries the typical parish, whether Catholic or Protestant, does not appear to be a community of the Holy Spirit.

Fresh theology of the Movements

There is another consideration. Preaching the gospel necessarily requires theology, since to speak about the Christian revelation presupposes that one has thought about it. And if we think of the earlier great movements of the Spirit, then it would be reasonable to expect the new movements to make their own contribution to the Church's theology. After all, there was first of all monastic theology, and afterwards the different schools of theology associated with the Franciscan, Dominican, and Jesuit charisms. One later order, the Redemptorists, has specialized in moral theology. It would, therefore, be wholly consistent with earlier movements to expect new theological developments to manifest themselves in connexion with movements such as Focolare, Communion and Liberation, and the Neo-catechumenate. And if this occurs, then this will have very concrete implications for the kind of evangelization that is practised. For how revelation is understood and what aspects are especially stressed, will inevitably affect the way the gospel is proclaimed. Nor is this merely of academic interest, insofar as the particular charism proves to contain some fresh insight into revelation, since we would naturally expect any such development to be highly relevant to an evangelization that is effective in our own time. In other words, any fresh theological approach will be of particular apostolic importance.

Papal endorsement of living Christian Communities

Pope John Paul II has clearly recognized the 'missionary dynamism' of the new movements. Already in 1990 he noted their 'rapid growth' in his encyclical Redemptoris Missio: '... they represent a true gift of God both for new evangelization and for missionary activity ... I therefore recommend that they be spread, and that they be used to give fresh energy, especially among young people, to the Christian life and to evangelization ...' (72) Eight years later at the 1998 congress, he pointed out the 'urgent need for powerful proclamation and solid, in-depth Christian formation' to counteract the 'secularized culture'. But the Pope went on to speak of another aspect of the movements, for preaching and education, as we have seen, are not enough in a dechristianized society: there was a 'great need for living Christian communities'. And the Pope's joy is palpable as he exclaimed, 'And here are the movements and the new ecclesial communities: they are the response, given by the Holy Spirit, to this critical challenge at the end of the millennium.' (222-3)

Here was the head of the college of bishops giving his authoritative endorsement: the new movements and communities are discerned to be the fruit of the Spirit. This is of the utmost importance, because, as *Lumen Gentium* stated, of the gifts of the Spirit 'the primacy belongs to the grace of the apostles to whose authority the Spirit himself subjects even those who are endowed with charisms'.(7) However, in the 1990 encyclical the Pope gave an implicit warning to both the movements and the local bishops: 'When these movements humbly seek to become part of the life of the local Churches', then they should (so the Pope implies) be 'welcomed by Bishops and priests within diocesan and parish structures'. (72)

New maturity of the Movements

By 1998 the Pope detected a new maturity in the movements. In his message to the congress at its opening, he
noted how from the beginning of his pontificate had
'given special importance to the progress of the ecclesial
movements', pointing to them 'as something new that is
still waiting to be properly accepted and appreciated'. He
went on to speak of their growing maturity: 'Today I
notice, with great joy, that they have a more mature self-
knowledge.' (16) It is as though the Pope recognized pub-
licly that the movements had come of age and left adolescence behind, adolescence with all its arrogance and
excesses. It is perhaps significant that he does not go on
to add that he has also noticed a growing appreciation on
the part of the local bishops and churches.

Tensions with the local Church

In his paper to the congress Cardinal Ratzinger warned
against any temptation on the part of any of the movements to imagine that they are the only way of understanding and living the gospel, but also recognized that
the local institutional church could also be to blame when
there was tension between the two. Indeed, it was 'almost
inevitable' that there would be conflict between 'the vitality' of a charismatic movement and 'the local community,
a conflict in which both sides may be at fault, and both
may be spiritually challenged'. At the end of his paper, as

in the Pope's address, one notes a sense that any fault now lies more with the local churches than with the movements, that is, if the space given to strictures against local bishops as against the movements is at all indicative. For Ratzinger speaks very emphatically and at length on the danger of local bishops and churches turning 'their own pastoral plans into the criterion of what the Holy Spirit is allowed to do', for 'an obsession with planning could render the Churches impervious to the action of the Holy Spirit'. The Cardinal's impatience with what he obviously perceives as an obstinate refusal to discern, let alone foster, the charisms of the Spirit is evident: 'Not everything should be fitted into the straightjacket of a single uniform organization; what is needed is less organization and more spirit!' It is not unheard of for local bishops to forbid or discourage a particular movement on the ground that it is divisive, as though that were justification enough. But Ratzinger rejects this argument, in which 'the highest pastoral value is attached to the avoidance of conflict', as actually being against the gospel: 'Faith remains a sword and may demand conflict for the sake of truth and love.' Ratzinger also vehemently rejects that 'attitude of intellectual superiority that immediately brands the zeal of those seized by the Holy Spirit and their uninhibited faith with the anathema of fundamentalism'. Of course, Ratzinger is not arguing that local bishops should have no say in the necessary discernment of charisms, but he is pointing out that the primacy of the petrine office should be respected by the episcopate when a new charismatic movement arrives on the scene - 'episcopacy can only preserve its dynamic and apostolic unity in subservience to primacy.' And, as he had earlier argued, it is the pope who has a special *episcope* or oversight over the whole Church and its mission and who has a special responsibility for maintaining the Church's missionary impetus world-wide.

In his address at the end of the 1998 congress, Pope John Paul II pointed out that the charisms given by the Holy Spirit are not only not independent of the sacraments which also come from the same Spirit but actually - if they are authentic - 'cannot but aim at the encounter with Christ in the sacraments'. And in an almost ecstatic passage, the Pope himself authenticates the charisms that have inspired the new ecclesial movements by affirming that this is exactly what he has witnessed in their intense sacramentality:

"The ecclesial realities to which you belong have helped you to rediscover your baptismal vocation, to appreciate the gifts of the Spirit received at Confirmation, to entrust yourselves to God's forgiveness in the sacrament of Reconciliation and to recognize the Eucharist as the source and summit of all Christian life. Thanks to this powerful ecclesial experience, wonderful Christian families have come into being which are open to life, true 'domestic churches,' and many vocations to the ministerial priesthood and the religious life have blossomed, as well as new forms of lay life inspired by the evangelical counsels. You have learned in the movements and new communities that faith is not abstract talk, nor vague religious sentiment, but new life in Christ instilled by the Holy Spirit." (223)

Internal renewal in the life of the local Church

We saw earlier how previous spiritual movements in the Church not only led to new apostolic and missionary initiatives but also to internal renewal in the life of the local churches. Thus, for example, in the sixteenth century the Jesuits provided a secular priesthood greatly in need of reform with a new model of the kind of disciplined and educated priest that was so needed in the face of the Protestant Reformation. There is every reason to hope that the same will be true of the ecclesial movements. Certainly, in the passage quoted above the Pope seems to think so. And there is no question that today not only marriage, but also priesthood and religious life are in a state of crisis. By concretely realizing the ecclesiology of Vatican II, the movements are putting before the Church a model of Christian communion in which the different parts of the Church form an organic and mutually supportive unity. Such a renewal of the life of the Church will lead to a renewal of all the states of the Christian life, whether marriage or priesthood or consecrated life. Of course, not every Catholic will belong to a movement, any more than all Catholics once became monks or friars or Jesuits. But just as those spiritual movements eventually affected the whole Church, so too the new ecclesial movements will profoundly change the Church of our time. They will help show the rest of the Church how 'the Church herself is a movement', to use Pope John Paul II's own description in his homily at the mass for the participants in the first international meeting of the movements in 1981. (109)

Note: Except where otherwise indicated, all references in brackets in the text are to the page numbers of: *Movements in the Church: Proceedings of the World Congress of the Ecclesial Movements, Rome, 27-29 May 1998* (Pontificium Consilium pro Laicis: Vatican City, 1999).